D0535276

DATE DUE

LEAD HIGH SCHOOL LIBRARY
320 S. MAIN ST.
LEAD, SD 57754-1548

6674-97

Police
Brutality

Look for these and other books in the Lucent
Overview series:

Abortion

Acid Rain

AIDS

Alcoholism

Animal Rights

The Beginning of Writing

Cancer

Child Abuse

Cities

The Collapse of the Soviet Union

Dealing with Death

Death Penalty

Democracy

Drugs and Sports

Drug Trafficking

Eating Disorders

Endangered Species

Energy Alternatives

Espionage

Extraterrestrial Life

Gangs

Garbage

The Greenhouse Effect

Gun Control

Hate Groups

Hazardous Waste

The Holocaust

Homeless Children

Illiteracy

Immigration

Money

Ocean Pollution

Oil Spills

The Olympic Games

Organ Transplants

Ozone

Pesticides

Police Brutality

Population

Prisons

Rainforests

Recycling

The Reunification of Germany

Smoking

Space Exploration

Special Effects in the Movies

Teen Alcoholism

Teen Pregnancy

Teen Suicide

The UFO Challenge

The United Nations

The U.S. Congress

Vanishing Wetlands

Vietnam

World Hunger

Zoos

Police Brutality

by Kelly C. Anderson

LUCENT
B·O·O·K·S

DISCARDED

LEAD HIGH SCHOOL LIBRARY
320 S. MAIN ST.
LEAD SD 57754-1548
66 74 - 97

LUCENT *Overview Series*

LUCENT *Overview Series*

Library of Congress Cataloging-in-Publication Data

Anderson, Kelly C. (Kelly Clark), 1962-
    Police brutality / by Kelly C. Anderson.
       p.   cm. — (Lucent overview series)
    Includes bibliographical references (p.   ) and index.
    ISBN 1-56006-164-2
    1. Police—United States—Complaints against—Juvenile
literature. 2. Civil rights—United States—Juvenile literature.
3. Violence (Law)—United States—Juvenile literature. [1. Police—
United States—Complaints against—Juvenile literature.
2. Police—Complaints against. 3. Civil rights.] I. Title. II. Series.
HV7936.C56A53   1995
363.2'32—dc20   94-9707
                                         CIP
                                        AC

No part of this book may be reproduced or used in any form or by any means, electrical,
mechanical, or otherwise, including, but not limited to, photocopy, recording, or any information storage and retrieval system, without prior written permission from the publisher.

Copyright © 1995 by Lucent Books, Inc.
P.O. Box 289011, San Diego, CA 92198-9011
Printed in the U.S.A.

Contents

Introduction

THE HIGHLY PUBLICIZED beating of Rodney King by uniformed police officers encouraged national debate on the issue of police brutality. The King incident caused people to question their own police departments. Gerald Williams, chief of police in Aurora, Colorado, and former president of the Police Executive Research Forum, a national professional organization, favors this debate. In congressional testimony in 1992, Williams said:

> We believe the King incident should be examined carefully. It should serve as a catalyst for self-examination for every city, large or small, every police or sheriff's department, and moreover, for every man and woman who carries a badge. We must ask ourselves hard questions: Are we fair? Are all of our citizens well served? Do we uphold the oaths we have taken to protect and serve?

Self-examination by police departments is not new. Police reform occurred throughout the country in the 1970s. At that time, the catalyst for change was also an act of police brutality. In the summer of 1968, youthful protesters at the Democratic National Convention in Chicago were met by police who beat them with clubs and seriously injured many. Although police brutality was not uncommon at the time, the Chicago incident was captured on film and broadcast to large numbers of viewers. This led to widespread

(Opposite page) Police brutality is not a new phenomenon. One well-publicized incident occurred during the Democratic National Convention in 1968 when police became overzealous in controlling antiwar protesters.

7

national concern about police brutality. Police departments responded by creating new standards of police professionalism.

Police professionalism, which considerably reduces police brutality, can be measured by improvements in several areas, including the requirements for becoming an officer, the training of new recruits, and the policies followed by individual departments. In the 1970s and 1980s, departments began requiring some college education for would-be officers, increased the number of mandatory training hours, and often increased the number of areas of police work in which training was available. In addition, most departments hammered out policies defining when and how officers could use physical force. Most police experts agree that these and other reforms contributed greatly to reductions in police brutality.

Although the catalyst for these reforms was an incident of police brutality, it was the police

Improved training has helped police improve professionalism and respond to problems with controlled strength. Here, Los Angeles police officers are trained in riot control techniques.

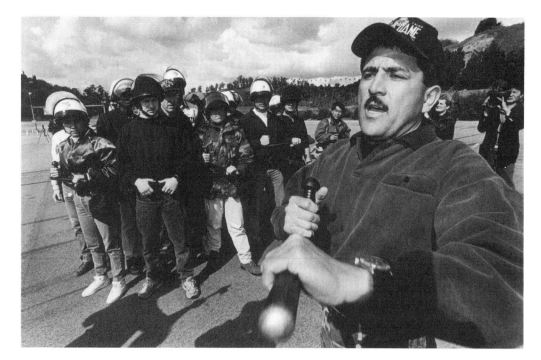

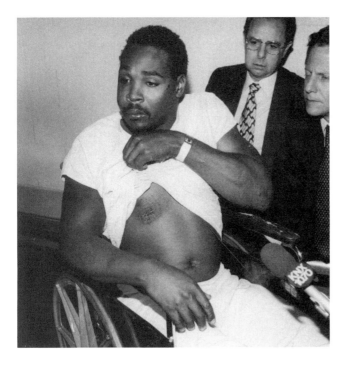

The film of Rodney King (left) being beaten by police officers returned the issue of police brutality to public attention.

themselves who directed and made the necessary changes. Police officers, like the rest of society, generally agree that brutality is bad and should not be tolerated. Former attorney general Richard Thornburgh said, "Responsible law enforcement officers condemn acts of police brutality by anyone in law enforcement. Those engaged in law enforcement must be among the first to assure the observance of the civil rights and civil liberties of all citizens."

The Rodney King video reminded the country that abuses of police authority continue. For some Americans, it was a shock just to learn that police brutality still exists. For police departments, it was a new challenge to their professionalism. The beating renewed national media attention to police brutality. The overriding message of the incident has been that constant examination is necessary, even in cities where the police are mostly good, mostly respectful of citizens' civil liberties.

1

The Use of Force

THE UNITED STATES prides itself on being a society ruled by law. The country is governed by a constitution, not by a king or by military might, and all citizens are expected to obey its laws, which are made by the people's elected representatives. No one, neither the president nor anyone else, is above the law. Moreover, a government based on the rule of law does not subject its citizens to the uncontrolled use of force.

Americans give their police the right to use physical force to protect the people who live by the laws that apply to all citizens. The police do not have an unlimited right to use unlimited force, however. Officers must follow laws and stick to policies that state how much force can be used in various situations. When police use unnecessary force, they may be breaking the law and committing police brutality.

(Opposite page) In their daily work, police officers often subdue violent individuals. Their difficult task is to accomplish this while remaining within the scope of the law.

Enforcing law and order

Citizens of the United States value law and order. No one wants the streets overrun by criminals who terrorize law-abiding people. Cities created police departments to prevent disorder

11

and investigate crime, and today these are primary tasks of all police departments.

The first police organizations in the United States were established in the nineteenth century, when big cities, such as New York, experienced large increases in violent crimes. These early police departments reflected the popular assumption that force was needed to control criminals and other lawless members of society. Even today, most citizens believe that if police are not allowed to use force, they will not be able to catch criminals or prevent crime. Former New York City police officer Harvey Schlossberg believes that force is often necessary to stop criminals. "The only thing some lawbreakers respect is force," writes Schlossberg in his 1974 book *Psychologist with a Gun*. "It is the way they have been brought up. As children they were beaten by their parents to make them obey, and as adults they obey only when authority is brutal. You cannot control some criminals unless you threaten them with force."

Most citizens agree that police must have the authority to use force, but most citizens do not

Early police departments such as this one in the 1880s were formed in cities as population and violent crime increased.

want police to use physical force in all situations. Police were intended to be different from the military, which uses deadly force against an enemy that threatens national interests. Police are generally expected to use limited force, when force is needed, although not against an enemy. John Alderson made this point even more clear in his 1985 book *The Listener:*

> The difference between the quasi-military and the civil policeman is that the civil policeman should have no enemies. People may be criminals, they may be violent, but they are not enemies to be destroyed. Once that kind of language gets into the police vocabulary, it begins to change attitudes.

This difference is very, very important. It is the major reason why police wear blue or brown uniforms—to distinguish them from the army, which wears green.

Police have the power to enforce laws and impose order, but they often do not have to use physical force to accomplish these tasks. Most police, in fact, do not use physical force on a typical day at work. Even police who more frequently are in situations that require physical force do not use it all day every day. The majority of American people do not need to be compelled forcefully to obey the law and respect the power of the police officer. For many men and women in police work, "law and order" is a relatively peaceful occupation.

How much force?

When force is needed, however, police are expected to use no more than is necessary to accomplish their jobs. To give a speeding ticket generally does not call for physical force, while apprehending an armed robber under conditions of hot pursuit might require the use or threat of deadly force.

14

Police departments provide guidelines about the amount of force their officers can use in various situations, and most have a policy of escalating force. This means that when officers begin interacting with a suspect, they are supposed to use the smallest amount of force appropriate for the circumstances; if this is not enough to bring the situation under control, officers may escalate, or increase, the force. There are six basic levels in police use of force.

The first level of force is the mere presence of the police. The presence of an officer is intimidating to most law-abiding people. Even people who are not in direct contact with an officer usually respond to police authority. For example, drivers slow down when they see a patrol car, and pedestrians are less likely to spit on the sidewalk or jaywalk in front of an officer.

Chicago police officers are trained in hand-to-hand combat and blocking techniques. This type of training teaches police how to protect themselves and how to use force appropriately.

The second level of force is verbalization. Verbalization actually has two stages: persuasive voice and command voice. Police use the generally polite, encouraging, persuasive voice in their normal interactions with citizens. The command voice is appropriate in more serious situations. An officer may command an uncooperative motorist to hand over his or her license, or command a fleeing purse snatcher to stop or freeze.

The next level of force is the firm grip. Police use a firm grip to physically communicate with a suspect or distressed citizen. An officer may use it to escort an uncooperative person into a squad car, for example. A firm grip, which does not cause pain, also may be used to encourage an emotionally distraught witness to stand still.

The fourth level of force is pain compliance, a serious escalation beyond the firm grip. With pain compliance, police may use fingerholds, wrist-locks, or other similar techniques that are

Police officers use a firm grip to enforce control and subdue a suspected drug dealer.

supposed to hurt. Police use pain compliance when suspects are physically uncooperative. For example, police may use pain compliance to break up a fistfight or to handcuff resistant suspects.

The fifth level of police force involves impact techniques. Impact techniques include kicking, hitting, and striking with a nightstick, as well as using Mace and Taser guns. Police resort to impact techniques when force is used against them. When the force against an officer is life-threatening, however, the use of deadly force becomes permissible.

The highest escalation of police force is the use of deadly force, which includes shooting with a gun as well as applying any other kind of force capable of killing or likely to kill a person. For

Impact techniques, such as the use of a nightstick to control a fleeing felon, are used only after other, less invasive, techniques fail.

example, hand-to-hand combat techniques can be used to halt blood flow to the brain or to block the passage of air into the lungs. Police may use deadly force to stop a fleeing felon who is armed and dangerous. Officers put their lives on the line, but they are not expected to die for the job if means of survival are available.

Although department policies usually require officers to use the minimum amount of force needed to take custody of a person and protect their own lives, officers have some discretion. The level of danger to police or bystanders will certainly influence the response. For example, an officer may approach the scene of an armed robbery in progress with gun drawn, prepared to use deadly force.

Excessive force

An officer who uses more force than policy allows is said to have used excessive force and may be guilty of police brutality, the excessive and lawless use of police force. Police brutality is a crime. Police officers who use excessive force are committing assault and battery. They may also be breaking other criminal laws that apply specifically to police officers. An officer can be arrested, tried, convicted, and imprisoned for committing police brutality.

When it does occur, police brutality can take many forms. Sometimes brutality takes the form of punishment. Police are expected to protect and serve; they are not supposed to punish. But police seemed to be administering summary punishment when they beat Adolph Archie to death in March 1992. Archie shot a police officer and was himself wounded, but living, when New Orleans officers arrested him, took him to a hospital, and did not present him for medical treatment. Instead, they waited in the parking lot

Guns drawn, police prepare to enter a crack house.

until they learned that their injured colleague had died. Then the officers took Archie away, beat him, and returned him to the hospital for medical treatment. Archie lived only twelve hours at the hospital, where he was found to have two skull fractures, a broken larynx, fractures of the cheekbones, and bleeding testicles; his teeth had been kicked in, and his entire body "exposed to blunt trauma."

Tactics and policy

At times brutality surfaces in the military tactics used by some police departments. Military tactics have become more common as police participate in their cities' wars on drugs and gangs, as was the case in 1986 in Los Angeles. The Jessie Larez family, which included Larez, his wife, seven children and grandchildren, was awakened one morning by a police raid. The police were searching for a gun they thought was in the Larez home, and they had a warrant. They did not knock or announce their presence, however. They burst into the Larez home, cursed and beat members of the family, and destroyed irreplaceable heirlooms. The gun was not found.

Although there have been times and places in the United States when police brutality was a typical occurrence, no police department today officially endorses this approach to law enforcement. No responsible police department formally instructs its officers to brutalize citizens. Some departments, though, typically use more or less force than is found in other cities. For example, for many years the Los Angeles Police Department (LAPD) listed chokeholds as intermediate force, while most departments viewed this technique as deadly force. But it is still rare to find that police brutality is standard practice in an entire police department.

Severe brutality was a routine method of law enforcement throughout the nineteenth century. In some areas, it was common for suspects to be pursued, caught, and hanged or shot without benefit of trial. In other areas, police routinely harassed and abused citizens because of their national origin or religion. In many areas, police routinely abused suspicious characters and suspects with whom they came into contact. These extreme uses of force continued as a matter of policy until the middle of the twentieth century.

The phrase "third degree" describes police officers' use of inhumane measures in the questioning of suspects. The third degree used to be quite common. Police routinely beat and tortured suspects with metal pipes, fists, and so on to elicit confessions. When complaints about the third degree arose in the 1930s, police began using bright, glaring lights and rubber

Police officers restrain a suspect in the late nineteenth century. Police of the time commonly used harsh methods for questioning suspects.

hoses, which did not leave marks on the suspect. These practices continued in most police departments through the 1960s. About 20 percent of midwestern police interviewed by researcher William Westley in 1951 admitted they would use force "to obtain information." Police experts believe the rates were much higher in places like New York City, which had a reputation for brutal interrogations.

Inadmissible confessions

A confession that has been forced from a suspect by means of torture is not admissible as evidence in court. People who are not guilty may confess just to stop the torture. Since, however, the third degree was usually conducted in secret, suspects could not call an attorney or anyone else for help. The secrecy also meant that no witnesses could testify later that a confession had been coerced instead of volunteered. Such confessions may or may not be true or factual, but police routinely offered them in court as evidence of voluntary admission of guilt.

Eventually, the courts, especially the U.S. Supreme Court under Chief Justice Earl Warren, forced police to abandon the routine use of brutality by refusing to admit forced confessions as evidence in trials. In 1966, in *Miranda v. Arizona*, the Supreme Court ruled on four cases that were being appealed because in each case the suspect had been held incommunicado (without being able to communicate with anyone other than the police officers involved) for many hours while police elicited a confession. In each case, the defendant's attorney argued that the confession should not be allowed as evidence in court because it had been obtained by police abusing their authority. Chief Justice Warren outlined the extreme abuses of police authority

found in the United States, especially in situations of police interrogations:

> In a series of cases decided by [the U.S. Supreme] Court . . . the police resorted to physical brutality—beating, hanging, whipping—and to sustained and protracted [lengthy] questioning incommunicado in order to extort confessions. The Commission on Civil Rights in 1961 found much evidence to indicate that "some policemen still resort to physical force to obtain confessions." The use of physical brutality and violence is not, unfortunately, relegated to the past or to any part of the country. Only recently in Kings County [Brooklyn], New York, the police brutally beat, kicked, and placed lighted cigarette butts on the back of a potential witness under interrogation for the purpose of securing a statement incriminating a third party.

The Court concluded that any time a citizen was in police custody being questioned as a suspect, police brutality was likely to occur. Thus it was impossible to know whether any given con-

The Supreme Court under Chief Justice Earl Warren (center) set new limits on the tactics used by police to arrest people and to obtain confessions.

fession was voluntary, as required by the rules of evidence. The Court addressed this problem by ruling that officers should explicitly advise every suspect that he or she has the right to remain silent and the right to have an attorney present during questioning. Courts now refuse to accept a confession unless it can be documented that a *Miranda* warning was given to the suspect before the confession was obtained. It is also necessary to have explained that anything a suspect says may be used against him or her in criminal proceedings.

Many citizens believe that *Miranda* hampers effective policing. They believe that brutal or intimidating interrogation is an important tool the police should be able to use to do their job. Many people fear that if suspects are encouraged to remain silent by the inability of police to use force obtaining confessions, many criminals will

An officer displays a Miranda card, which states a suspect's rights upon arrest. Police must read suspects their rights before making an arrest.

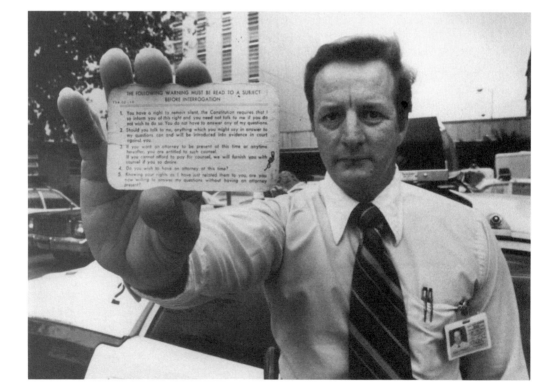

go free. Despite criticism, *Miranda* has effectively protected the rights of suspects. Prior to *Miranda*, the third degree was one of the most common forms of police brutality. After *Miranda*, the police were no longer allowed to question suspects privately, and had to be able to prove that confessions were voluntary. The reduction of physical abuse of suspects by police is directly related to the *Miranda* decision, a turning point in the history of police brutality.

Brutality persists

Brutality is decreasing by historical standards. It is no longer the standard police method for dealing with criminals and suspects. However, police brutality continues to exist. Some individual officers routinely engage in brutality, and some police departments condone it.

The U.S. Department of Justice investigates civil rights violations in cases of police brutality. Between 1985 and 1991, the Justice Department received fifteen thousand formal complaints of brutality. The Justice Department investigates about twenty-five hundred of these cases each year. In thousands of cases investigated during the 1980s, the federal government found that police from many areas of the country engaged in kidnapping, beating, and homicide to perform their jobs.

Many of these investigations resulted in police convictions. For example, a county sheriff in West Virginia was convicted in 1983 of beating to death a handcuffed suspect with a flashlight. A Honolulu police officer was convicted in 1984 because he forced a suspect into a watery ditch and made him "catch toads with his mouth." The Justice Department prosecuted for brutality an Ohio police officer who had punched a woman in the mouth and then filed false charges against her. The officer was convicted in 1989 by a federal jury for his brutality. Every state and every major city has confirmed incidents of police brutality.

The severity of brutality varies. Sometimes, as in the case of Adolph Archie, it results in death. Sometimes the injured citizen suffers broken bones or minor wounds. At other times, the victim of police brutality may have only scratches or bruises. Regardless of the severity of the injury, an act of brutality is not acceptable.

Taking liberty

Police swear to uphold, protect, and defend the Constitution of the United States as well as their respective state constitutions. Aurora, Colorado, police chief Gerald Williams has expressed this obligation concisely: "Law enforcement exists to protect the values of society as demanded by the Constitution."

Police brutality violates the constitutional rights of the victims, and therefore, many argue, puts the rights of all citizens at risk. In an article published in the *Nation*, Kim Bendheim, a resident of Los Angeles, expressed a feeling common to many people. "This is America," said Bendheim, "and in this country, so I was told, we have rights, among them, one would hope, the right not to be harassed, beaten or shot by our own police." If police are allowed to do this to some citizens, people fear they may abuse the rights of any citizen.

Federal law makes it a crime for police to deprive a person of his or her protected rights. The constitutionally protected rights concerned in police brutality were listed by former assistant attorney general John Dunne when he addressed a congressional hearing in 1991. These constitutional rights include, said Dunne, "the right to be free from unwarranted assaults, the right to be kept free from harm while in official custody, the right to be free from illegal arrests and illegal searches, and the right to be free from deprivation of property without due process of law."

Although police brutality is against the law, the law does not clearly state when "acceptable force" crosses the line into brutality. The American Civil Liberties Union (ACLU) is an organization devoted to maintaining the constitutional rights of individuals. The ACLU wants all police departments to adopt clearly defined, limited policies regarding the use of force.

Others worry that such policies would make the job of the police more difficult than it already

Harrington/People's Daily World.

"Don't worry, chief, we'll find something—they don't call us crack cops for nothing."

Some citizens worry about limits that might disrupt a police force's ability to protect law-abiding citizens. Others say clearly defined rules must be adopted to prevent use of excessive force.

is. They want to keep limits on use of force flexible because they believe that police must be able to decide on a fitting course of action based on the events unfolding before them. If police were not allowed such discretion, they would have less freedom to handle each situation individually. Many people fear that this would put police in a weaker position than lawbreakers, and make all of society more vulnerable to crime.

People today are so fearful that crime will strike their homes and take over their neighborhoods that many are willing to give police more leeway, even if it means the possibility of police using greater force. This idea was expressed by one woman who lived in a high-crime neighborhood: "We'd rather have the police be too brutal than too easy." Police have a difficult, dangerous job, and they confront dangerous people who are often in crisis. Many people believe that to be

Reprinted by permission: Tribune Media Services.

effective and to protect their own lives, police are going to have to use force sometimes. But this does not resolve the recurring question: At what point does force become brutality?

2

Police Point
of View

THE NATURE OF POLICE WORK shapes the attitudes and viewpoints of police officers. The police officer's job is psychologically and emotionally demanding; sometimes it entails violence, and generally it revolves around crisis. Society calls on police to handle a wide range of problems, including minor traffic accidents, murder investigations, family fights, muggings, house burglaries, carjackings, lost children, and crowd control at concerts.

Police are in a unique position. They see the best and the worst of American society. Day in and day out, police officers encounter individuals who break traffic laws, harass strangers, and commit assaults. But they also encounter people who report neighborhood crime, come to the aid of strangers, and provide social services for children and adults in crisis. They see some of the most horrible and most wonderful parts of their society. An ACLU manual attempts to define this unique position and to describe some of its effects:

(Opposite page) The average police officer spends most of his or her time helping people in distress. But policing also places officers in violent and life-threatening situations.

Police work is multifaceted, stressful, difficult, and dangerous. Moreover, constant confrontation with the human face of our country's most severe social problems almost inevitably engenders in

29

some officers such a dim view of the public they are supposed to serve that they eschew completely the role of "servant" for that of "warrior."

To protect and serve

Most people do think of police officers as warriors or crime fighters, but their mission—to protect and serve—includes service to the community above and beyond stopping crime. Officers who work in densely populated, high-crime areas have different experiences from officers working less populous, more rural communities. In general, though, the average police officer spends more of his or her time in service work than in crime-related activities. "At least 80 percent of police work involves answering calls for help that have nothing to do with crime," writes Anthony Bouza in his book *The Police Mystique: An Insider's Look at Cops, Crime, and the Criminal Justice System.* Bouza is a twenty-four-year veteran of the New York City Police Department who later was the chief of police in Minneapolis. "They involve rescues, medical emergencies, and the scores of other [calamities] that attend the human situation far more often than even the much heralded and feared crimes and acts of violence."

Patrolling and paper work take up a lot of an officer's day. Police may make minor arrests or spend time monitoring traffic and giving tickets to people who are speeding or violating other traffic laws. Much of the typical day, however, consists of responding to 911 calls for help with a variety of problems. Some 911 calls are crime related, but many more are from people who need assistance because of an accident or illness, or to cope with a nuisance. For example, a caller to 911 may want the police to check on an elderly relative who has not answered the phone and may have fallen or died, or to ask a neighbor to move a car blocking a driveway.

The calls for help in large cities are so numerous that in many police departments these requests must be prioritized. One of the largest expectations that citizens place on police is fast response to emergency calls. If police gave equal weight to all 911 calls, they would not be available to react quickly to emergencies. Therefore, in some cities, the 911 operators give priority status to calls about crimes in progress or accidents on major highways. In such a system, calls that do not require a police officer to respond, such as a report of a stolen bicycle, may be handled over the phone. Regardless of whether a city prioritizes its 911 calls, its service function continues to account for most of the daily tasks of its officers.

Police officers play many roles in their service to the community. The officers' tasks are as

Much of a police officer's day is spent in routine patrols, handing out traffic citations, and completing paper work.

varied as the calls for help. As writer David Kupelian explains in *New Dimensions* magazine, "Police must play the role of combat soldier, referee, psychologist, urban negotiator, social worker, doctor, and older brother. To do this, they must be supermen."

Dangerous job

Although police work is dominated by service and helping people, the job description also includes life-and-death risks of crime fighting. Veteran Santa Monica officer Gary Steiner describes the stress and risk police officers experience on every shift: "Very often officers are put into situations where one minute everything is fine and the next second, literally, you are going to be killed unless you act."

Friends and family pay their last respects to a New York detective killed in the line of duty. Every year, about 150 officers die while on the job.

Every year, many police officers are injured seriously or fatally while performing their work. About 150 officers are killed nationwide each year in the line of duty. In 1993 alone, 7 Los Angeles area officers were killed on the job. Tens of thousands are assaulted annually—as many as 80,000 reported by the FBI crime statistics in 1992. This condition is an integral part of the job, and officers know that at any time they could become one of those wounded or killed.

Most law enforcement professionals know or know of a fellow officer who has been injured or killed in the line of duty. Most of the time, these casualties occur in tense, fast-moving situations. Domestic violence calls, crimes in progress, and hot pursuit of suspects in shootings are among the most dangerous situations for officers. In all such cases, and similar ones, the suspect has already resorted to unlawful violence.

For example, a Culver City, California, police officer was shot in the neck in February 1994 while in pursuit of two armed robbery suspects. The officer and his partner chased the suspects by car until the suspects' vehicle crashed. The chase resumed on foot. It was during this pursuit that one suspect shot the officer.

Death and injury

Not all police shootings occur during a chase or a highly emotional situation, however. Sometimes officers are injured in routine, seemingly harmless situations—such as an officer who approaches a vehicle to give a speeding ticket and is shot at close range. In Missouri, for example, several officers have been assaulted in traffic stop situations. Missouri Highway Patrol trooper Jimmie Linegar was shot to death south of Branson, Missouri, in 1985. Linegar and his partner were conducting a routine spot check, directing

This police officer was paralyzed by a bullet during a shoot-out. Such confrontations make officers extremely cautious.

passing vehicles to the shoulder to permit a brief inspection of drivers' licenses and vehicle condition. After pulling over a van driven by David Tate and running a check on his license, the Missouri officers approached the vehicle from either side. Tate, a member of a white supremacist group called the Covenant of the Sword and the Arm of the Lord, opened fire on Linegar with an automatic weapon.

Two years later, Missouri trooper Russell Harper was also shot to death east of Springfield. Harper was conducting routine radar surveillance on U.S. Highway 60 when he saw a pickup truck exceeding the speed limit. Harper pursued and motioned the truck to pull over. The truck turned off onto a side road to stop. As Harper pulled his car up behind, the driver of the truck got out and sprayed automatic weapon fire across the trooper's car.

Because their physical safety can be compromised at any time, most officers approach every situation with caution, realizing that it could become deadly. Police know that they are vulnerable to life-and-death risks, and this knowledge affects the way they interpret situations, approach suspects, and react to perceived danger. Rookie Los Angeles officer Samuel Rhone described his own reaction to the life-and-death risk by saying that people need to understand the officer's right to protect himself, and "if they approach officers in a threatening way with a weapon, there's a likelihood they'd get shot. You don't want to overreact, but if your life is threatened, you have to take appropriate action."

Stressful job

The life-and-death risks of crime fighting produce high levels of stress in police work. Responding to emergency calls creates physical symptoms of stress. Heart rate and adrenaline levels increase tremendously in officers who respond to calls of recently committed crimes or crimes in progress. Life-threatening situations are not the only causes of stress for officers, though.

Police stress is also created by constant exposure to people who are angry, desperate, and in pain. Officers frequently respond to calls for help in which the underlying social problem cannot be cured by police intervention. For example, a neighborhood corner may be plagued with loud, boisterous crowds of unemployed adults or teenagers, or a resident may call the police because a drunk keeps appearing in the doorway, demanding to be let in. In many situations, the officer may be able to alleviate the current crisis, but a single arrest is not likely to resolve the problem.

Part of the stress of a job in law enforcement is often the result of facing thousands of situations a year that bring the officer face to face

An officer uses a machine called a stress simulator. Training on such machines is supposed to lower an officer's anxiety and improve his or her reflexes in stressful situations.

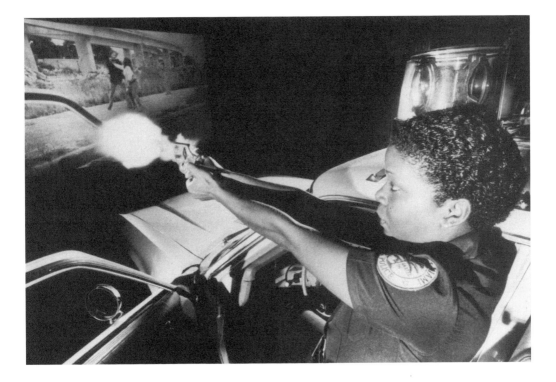

Police attempt to calm a man in deep distress. Officers never know what or who they will encounter when responding to such calls.

with examples of the country's biggest problems. More than most other people, police see and experience the tragic results of alcoholism, drug abuse, chronic unemployment, poverty, mental illness, and domestic violence.

The police officer's job is to respond to people in trouble, whether it involves a crime or an emergency of another kind. Some officers are better prepared than others for dealing with these sad circumstances of American life, whether by training, by maturity, by an inborn sense of how to work with people, or by all these characteristics. Edwin J. Delattre, the author of *Character and Cops: Ethics in Policing*, believes most people who become police officers are prepared to deal with these stresses. According to Delattre, "Most police around the country do not have a bunker mentality. They go on forces knowing what they'll have to put up with; they like their jobs and are ready and able to stand the pressure."

But the stresses of policing do affect some officers. Some adjust badly to the daily pressures of police work. Delattre explains:

> They are ground down by danger, resentment of criminals who prosper, perceived failure of social service and criminal agencies, and the daunting

repetitiveness of their work. Some drift toward despair over the violence, suffering, hopelessness, ignorance, and self-destructive behavior they encounter day after day. Some are ineffective— even dangerous—because they become cynical, convinced that policing is a daily battle of "us against them."

The stresses of the job often spill over into an officer's personal and family life. "The level of violence against officers has led to more alcoholism, more suicides, more broken homes," reported Faye Fiore and Miles Corwin of the *Los Angeles Times* in 1994. "More law enforcement couples require counseling today than ever before."

To help officers deal with stress, many police departments offer counseling services. Most of the programs are similar to employee assistance programs available from any major company or institution: they offer individual counseling, referrals to twelve-step programs, and substance abuse recovery support. These programs are important because, many police administrators believe, officers are not likely to seek counseling outside the department.

Police culture

While some officers find comfort and help in counseling, nearly all of them get their greatest support from coworkers. The stress and the danger of police work are two of the biggest factors leading police officers to bond together and form a unique culture of their own. Many police feel they must depend on each other, not civilians, and certainly not criminals. A family of police, or fellowship, is formed based on the need to trust and depend on other officers.

One reason for this strong relationship is the belief by most officers that only other members of the police force know and understand the job

© Germano/Rothco. Reprinted with permission.

and the nature of the work. In *The Police Mystique*, author Anthony Bouza says that the police profession remains a mystery to outsiders. "Cops are welded together by dangerous experiences and shared secrets that produce a strong bonding effect," writes this seasoned officer and administrator. "Theirs is an institution that, despite being on permanent public display, has successfully resisted intrusion and study."

Police officers share similar and relatively unique experiences, which lead them to stick together even in their social lives. One officer said that when he tried to associate with outsiders, someone would inevitably make a derogatory or insulting comment, so he felt more comfortable around other people in police work. In his book, Anthony Bouza says that such social exclusivity is common: "They work around the clock and begin to socialize mostly with other cops, usually members of their own squad. . . . The brotherhood in blue . . . inspires a fierce and unquestioning loyalty to all cops, everywhere."

British police scholar Robert Reiner, who believes that this brotherhood carries a mission, said, "This is the feeling that policing is not just a job, but a way of life with a worthwhile purpose, at least in principle."

Although the brotherhood serves a supportive function, experts like Bouza warn that it also can increase narrow-mindedness, serving to distance officers from the rest of society. Harvey Goldstein, a psychologist who worked with the police department in Prince George's County, Maryland, believes that this brotherhood can be self-destructive and antisocial:

> The police subculture says, "We're special, we have an enigma [mystery] about us. We're different." That difference is the problem. It reinforces machismo, the territorial ethic. On an international level, we see that one thing that keeps nations together is a common enemy. That's what's happening here. Only here the common enemy isn't just criminals; it's the community at large.

Code of silence

One feature that defines police culture is the code of silence, an unwritten rule among police officers that no officer will make damaging statements about other officers. The code has existed for much of police history. Every working police officer knows it exists, and many follow it absolutely. William Westley's studies of secrecy and the police in the late 1950s found that eleven of fifteen officers would not report another officer for taking money from a prisoner. Only one of those eleven said he would testify against the officer if the prisoner complained. Many officers believe that the basic bonds of trust would be weakened by breaking the silence.

The code of silence has never been written into departmental policy, however. "Cops are never told to be silent or to keep the agency's secrets," writes Anthony Bouza. "They never see an order upholding the code of silence that guides their working lives. There is no need to be explicit." Bouza also says, in *The Police Mystique*, that rookies are initiated into the code of silence along with other rules of the brotherhood.

Cracking the silence

Police experts believe that the code of silence enabled officers to hide corruption and brutality for most of police history. In the last few decades of this century, however, a growing desire for police professionalism has encouraged officers to speak out when their colleagues commit crimes. This does not mean that all police officers will now break the code of silence, but it does mean that an increasing number will not follow the

Police develop a strong and lasting camaraderie with one another. They may feel that no one understands them except their fellow officers.

code to the extent of protecting those who commit illegal acts.

Rookie Los Angeles officer Samuel Rhone believes that the code of silence would not prevent him from reporting abuse of authority:

> I became a police officer to uphold the law, not to break it, and if I saw something [illegal], I'd take appropriate action. In the long run, it would help the department, not hurt it. The fact that it would be known this type of activity was not tolerated would help the trust between us and the community.

Joseph McNamara agrees that while the code of silence is powerful, it can be cracked. He has seen it happen to break police corruption. Interviewed in 1984 by Nikki Meredith for *Psychology Today*, former San Jose, California, police chief McNamara said:

> The cops themselves became so opposed to it, they started reporting it. We are beginning to see the same thing happen with abuse of authority. Like corruption, once you hold excessive force up to the light, no one can defend it, not even cops.

Survival

Although police officers work in a troubled and violent world, a world often shunned by much of society, their mission to protect and serve does not justify brutality, and most officers do not condone or practice brutality. Don Edwards, who represents a California district in Congress, expressed a common opinion:

> Police work is dangerous, difficult, and often unappreciated, but there is no excuse for the type of behavior recorded on video tape in Los Angeles. Seeing [Rodney King] being beaten was offensive to all Americans, particularly to the tens of thousands of dedicated law enforcement officers who would not engage in such conduct.

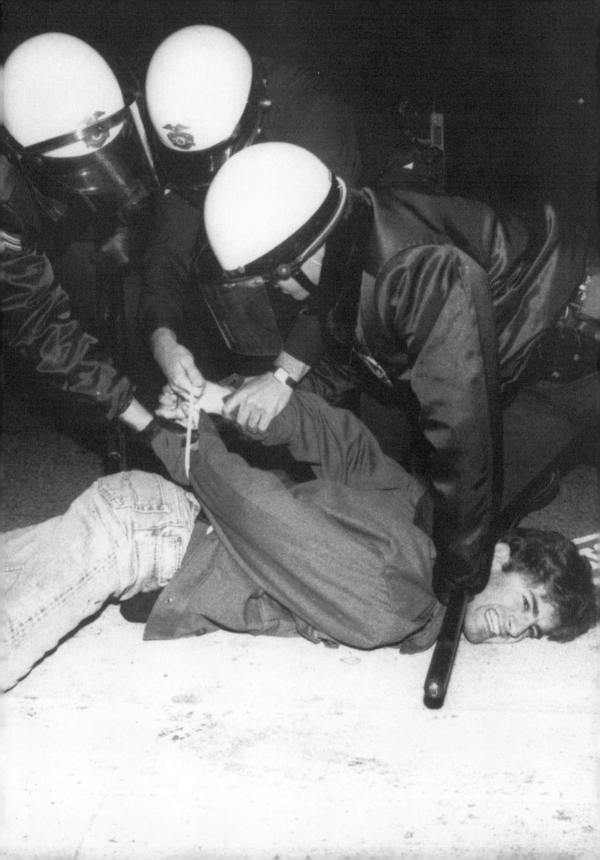

3

Crossing the Line

POLICE OFTEN ARE SEEN as a thin blue line of protection between criminals and law-abiding citizens, but when police use excessive force, they cross the line and become one of the criminals. Brutality incidents, evidence that police do cross that line, continue to happen all over the country, from New York City to Dayton, Ohio, to San Antonio, Texas, to Los Angeles, California.

Yet, many officers never cross the line that separates acceptable force from brutality. Many officers understand the pressures and demands of their jobs and find ways to cope with both forms of stress in a professional and acceptable manner. In some cities, entire departments have never had complaints of police brutality. Edwin Delattre points out that many officers typically react with restraint. In *Character and Cops*, he writes:

> I have seen police officers injured because they limited their use of force against wildly violent individuals, and I have seen them refrain from using deadly force even in life-threatening situations. Many police feel anguish after using fully justified force; few take pleasure in it, let alone react with glee.

What causes police officers to cross the line? There is no single, clear-cut answer. Most experts

(Opposite page) A defiant protester is arrested outside a political fundraising event. Research shows that defiance often precedes police abuse of force.

43

agree that the forces that push some officers over the line are as complex and multifaceted as police work itself. Some blame the job, saying that police violence is a natural outgrowth of the violent world in which officers work. Others cite personal problems, badly drawn up departmental policies, community and political pressures, and poor supervision as underlying causes of police brutality. Research has also shown that certain actions or events often precede or trigger brutal behavior by police.

Defiant attitude

Defiance of any kind can trigger police abuse because defiance is a challenge or threat. A defiant person may be disobeying an officer's commands or resisting his or her authority. A defiant person is also not cooperating, and uncooperative people are suspicious to police. Many people—including police—believe that anyone who fails to cooperate with police must have something to hide. Officers who interpret defiance as a threat to police authority may be more likely to escalate force quickly.

A young man taunts police, a sign of disrespect for the authority of the officers.

Police officers see defiance in many forms. People who have committed crimes typically defy police instructions. Yet citizens who claim their constitutional rights (such as travelers who will not permit their suitcases to be searched without a warrant) or become irritated with police priorities (such as traffic offenders who ask why officers are not out chasing real criminals) may also be viewed by police as defiant. Defiance does not always lead to brutality. But police researchers have found that when police brutality occurs, an act of defiance has usually preceded it.

When defiance leads to abuse

While many officers find ways of responding to defiance without resorting to brutality, some officers lack the skills or maturity to maintain control of events without the use of excessive force. Under these circumstances, defiance may lead to abuse. This is apparently what happened to Byron Gillum in November 1989. Houston police officer Scott Tschirhart reported that Gillum's car slowed to ten miles per hour after the squad car pulled in behind him. The officer considered this behavior suspicious and stopped Gillum for not wearing a seat belt. Tschirhart reported that when he approached the vehicle, the twenty-four-year-old Gillum implied that the officer "was stopping him just to harass him," and that Tschirhart should be out chasing "real criminals."

Angered by Gillum's attitude, Tschirhart called in Gillum's license number to see if there were outstanding warrants or other pending charges against Gillum. When the dispatcher reported none, the officer said, "Please say you have something on Gillum . . . bad attitude." Tschirhart returned to Gillum's car, where he later reported he thought he saw a gun, although in fact Gillum was not armed. Tschirhart opened fire while Gillum scrambled to get out the other side of his car. Gillum was killed with eight bullets in his body, four of which entered from his back.

The high-speed chase

One form of defiance, the high-speed chase, has been linked frequently to brutality. Where brutality occurs, a high-speed chase has often preceded it. In the now famous Rodney King case, for example, King had led several officers in high-speed pursuit. According to court testimony, once King stopped, he was stung with a Taser gun and repeatedly beaten with clubs. He suffered facial cuts and a split lip as well as "nine skull fractures, a cracked cheekbone, a smashed eye socket, and a broken leg."

Officers explain that the high-speed chase is one of the most stressful situations an officer

A large photo of Rodney King clearly shows injuries inflicted by police. King led police in a high-speed chase before being caught. Such chases are stressful and dangerous and have been linked to brutality.

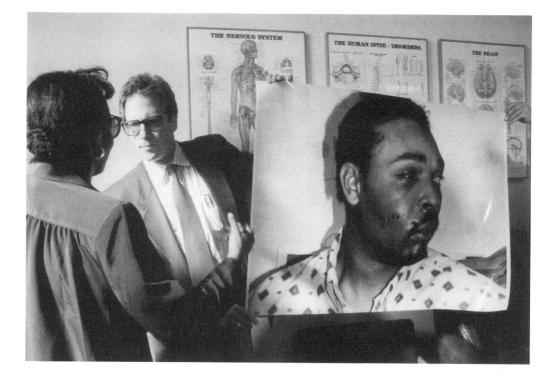

faces. One stress is the chase itself; driving a car at high speed requires focus, skill, and strength. The chase also creates the stress of potential consequences. A high-speed chase can kill or injure innocent drivers and pedestrians, damage property, and create other disasters along its path.

A high-speed chase also threatens a police officer's authority. Instead of pulling over when the lights and siren came on, the suspect driver has increased speed to flee from the officer. This is similar to resisting arrest. So in addition to being stressful, the high-speed chase can make an officer angry because the suspect's failure to cooperate may be seen as an insult. Like other forms of defiance, fleeing from the police at high speeds creates an assumption or suspicion that the person making the getaway has done something wrong and might be dangerous.

By the time an officer catches a suspect driver, the officer is likely to be stressed and angry, with his or her adrenalin level high and heart rate fast. One veteran Austin, Texas, police sergeant described feelings he and some of his colleagues have experienced in high-speed chases:

> You get real, real frightened in the chase. And it's like you gotta vent that, and either you're at a level where you can vent it without hurting somebody—or you hurt somebody. Somebody gives you an excuse, you know, he'll swing at you, won't do what you tell him to do, he'll reach for something and do something he shouldn't do. He gets hurt.

Paramilitary force

Defiance alone can provoke brutal police behavior. More often, however, other conditions exist to create an atmosphere in which brutality can occur. The militarization of the police, some experts suggest, contributes to police brutality. Militarization occurs when the police take on the role and tactics of an occupying army rather than a civil peace-keeping force. In the wars on drugs and gangs mandated by politicians in the 1980s, police departments were empowered to use extraordinary means to accomplish the task of reducing drug- and gang-related crime. Many critics argue that such political mandates create a siege mentality that leads police to think they can use any means necessary, including abuse of citizens' rights, to catch criminals.

Military tactics

Some police departments have adopted military tactics, such as surprise attacks and battle planning, to combat drugs and gangs. In the 1980s, militarization became more common, and the results were often mixed. Although some cities reported high arrest rates from these tactics, many police departments also faced charges of excessive force. For example, in a gang-related raid in 1988, which was described as a search-and-destroy mission by one attorney, about seventy Los Angeles Gang Task Force officers descended on four apartments in the South-Central section of the city. Three days before the raids, senior officers announced at a roll call that the apartments should be made uninhabitable. When police went to the apartments, they chopped up the insides with axes, pulled toilets from the floor, left water running in faucets, cut phone wires, and pulled out lighting fixtures. Some officers spray-painted "LAPD Rules" on the walls of the destroyed apartments.

The residents were terrorized by police and humiliated by physical abuse, such as being made to lie face down on the ground for hours. According to Jerome Skolnick and James Fyfe, the authors of *Above the Law*, reporter Joe

Domanick wrote that the thirty-three people found in the apartments "were forced to whistle the theme from the old Andy Griffith television show, and to run a gauntlet of police officers who allegedly struck them with fists and flashlights." When such military tactics are deployed against citizens, police officers have crossed the line from acceptable to excessive force.

The image of a militarized police department concerns many experts. Colorado police chief Gerald Williams is one of many experts disturbed by the image of a militarized police force. In 1992 congressional hearings he said:

> The war on drugs and the arms race we have waged with drug dealers reinforces the Rambo-like image of police officers. It is an image that professional departments discourage. The attitude that all is fair in war has [added to] the misconception that police are an occupying army that should do whatever is necessary to apprehend criminals.

The militarization of police is repugnant to many experts. "I think the whole notion of police as soldiers in a war is something that has to be changed," said James Fyfe, a sixteen-year veteran

Bill Garner, © 1991, The Washington Times. Reprinted with permission.

of the New York City Police Department (NYPD) and now a professor of police administration. Fyfe believes the image must be changed because "the war model of policing encourages police violence of the type that victimized Rodney King." Many police and police experts agree with Fyfe. Most citizens do not want the police to see the people in their community as the enemy in a war.

Practice or custom

Researchers who study police abuse have found that officers may be more likely to commit brutality when it is the practice or custom of their precinct, unit, or department. These practices are not written policy, but may develop over time as senior officers ignore or reinforce brutal behavior.

© 1991 International copyright by Cartoonews Inc., N.Y.C., USA

Hand in Hand

When senior officers fail to discipline those responsible for incidents of police brutality, or when they directly or indirectly encourage excessive force, it is more likely that individual officers will resort to brutality. Wade Henderson, an executive with the Washington, D.C., office of the National Association for the Advancement of Colored People (NAACP), explained that investigation into one complaint of brutality in a city usually produces information about a pattern of excessive force:

> In many instances when [we] go into a community, we don't see merely one police abuse incident. What we see are a pattern [and] a history of police abuse incidents. And, in fact, in many instances these incidents actually increase over time because many of the perpetrators of the violence feel that they indeed [are permitted] to conduct these actions.

One example of a pattern of practicing excessive force was found in the borough of Queens, in New York City. In the 1980s, the 106th precinct house in Queens became known as the "torture precinct" because of the brutal police handling of suspects. One such suspect was eighteen-year-old Mark Davidson, who said he was walking down the street when six police officers "nabbed" him. The officers took him to the 106th, where they used an electric stun gun to inflict pain and forty burn marks on his body until he said that he had sold $10 worth of marijuana. Three other victims of brutality at the 106th came forward after Davidson's case was made public. An investigation revealed that brutality was a regular practice at the Queens precinct. Although use of brutality was contrary to official policy of the NYPD at the time, the precinct commanding officer knew that it was occurring and approved. Investigators found that rookie officers in the 106th precinct were routinely trained by experienced coworkers

Mark Davidson (right) brought the issue of brutality at the 106th precinct in New York City to public light. Davidson was burned with an electric stun gun by officers attempting to extract a confession from him.

in the use of brutal methods to perform their job.

The Queens precinct is not the only police force to come under fire for brutalizing citizens. Many critics accused the Los Angeles Police Department of routinely using excessive force when it was under the direction of Police Chief Daryl Gates. Allegations of routine violence also have been made against departments in Philadelphia, Miami, Washington, D.C., Houston, and Detroit. Citizens and leaders of most of these and other cities have demanded major reforms in their police departments after routine brutality was disclosed.

Often, these reforms did not happen early enough, as Jerome Skolnick and David Bayley explain in their book *The New Thin Blue Line: Police Innovation in Six American Cities:*

> That the Houston Police Department was long overdue for change was obvious to almost everyone. The misdeeds of the Houston police had

become a scandal of national proportions by the end of the 1970s. The Houston police officer was seen, newspaperman Rick Nelson reported, as "someone who'd bust your head open and ask questions later."

The Houston Police Department began major reforms in the 1980s after it acknowledged a history of department-wide abuses, including brutality.

The bad egg

Although brutality is most likely to occur in departments or precincts where senior officers ignore it or give it their approval, brutality can be found in departments that work hard to prevent it. Individuals who violate departmental policies and abuse their authority as police officers are sometimes known as "bad eggs." Most police researchers and experts believe that the "bad egg" officer is relatively rare.

Most big-city police departments use psychological tests and personal interviews to screen

A trainee takes a test to prove her psychological and personal suitability to police work.

applicants and recruits in hopes of eliminating those who are not fit for the job. These tests usually identify people with major character disorders, such as pathological lying, or mental illnesses, such as schizophrenia. The tests are not perfect, however, and some people may be selected to serve who are not mentally or emotionally capable of the demands of police work. Many departments, however, do not even use these tests. Preemployment screening is expensive, and some departments cannot afford it. Many departments are so small that they do not see a need for special testing.

Weeding out problems

Police departments that use screenings are more likely to hire officers who are fit for the job. Rookie Los Angeles officer Pamela Pitcher believes her department's new screening process is effective. "The screening now, the psychological testing, would weed out the people who have [brutal, violent] tendencies," she said. "The person who wants to walk around in a uniform and tell people what to do is just not going to get in." Departments that do not prescreen applicants may risk putting an officer on the streets who is already a violent person, more likely to brutalize suspects than members of a group that passed the screening.

An officer who resorts to brutality may be venting frustrations with the job or even with his or her personal life. One of the typical frustrations police face is that after they catch criminals, the courts often let them go. Attorney Paul Chevigny refers to police brutality as "summary punishment," because it often takes the form of administering justice without the benefit of the courts. In an article in *Time* magazine, Richard Lacayo explained this behavior: "The temptation to administer street-corner sentences is some-times reinforced by the frustration of knowing that many of those the police collar will get off on plea bargains or serve mockingly short sentences."

Most police departments discipline officers who are found to have commited brutality. Depending on the offense, discipline may range from a reprimand to dismissal from the force. In some departments, complaints against officers are kept on file. Although a single offense seldom is enough to justify firing, a record of repeated brutal behavior may allow police officials to weed their departments of problem officers. Chief Ernie Barbee, who commands a small police department in Missouri, fired an officer because of a pattern of abuses that had been uncovered. "No one offense would have led to firing," said Barbee, who believes that discipline is the most effective way to stop police abuses.

No bright line

Whether an officer has crossed the line into brutality is a question that must be answered on a case-by-case basis, with all the circumstances of the situation considered. There is no bright line that clearly says what is and what is not permissible. Even when there is agreement on the basic events, perceptions of those events greatly affect whether the incident is determined to be brutality or justified force. The case of Lorenzo Colston offers an example of just how different perceptions can be.

On the night of September 29, 1993, Colston was riding in a car driven by a man named Marcus Fields when police pulled the car over for a defective headlight. One of the officers arrested Fields after discovering that he was wanted in connection with an old speeding ticket. The officer also interviewed Colston, who was drunk.

An antiwar protester resists attempts by police to arrest him. Officers may become increasingly violent when trying to deal with such resistance.

The officer later testified that he did not believe that Colston had given his right name and age. He decided to arrest Colston at this point and ordered Colston to kneel on the ground. Colston testified that he did not know he was under arrest and did not understand why he was ordered to the ground. When Colston did not act quickly, the officer again ordered him to kneel. Colston did as he was told. Then the officer took out his club, and told Colston to cross his feet. Already on his knees, Colston tried to cross his feet, and asked why he was being treated this way. The officer said, "You won't tell us who you are when you been asked." Colston told the officer his real name then, but the officer ordered him to "get on the ground."

Colston went to all fours, but did not drop his chest to the ground. A second officer grabbed him by the shoulders and the first officer began clubbing Colston. Colston moved forward to avoid the blows, then standing, he struggled with the officers who continued shouting "Get down. Get down. Get down," while they clubbed him. Colston tried to deflect blows with his forearms and tried to grab the clubs away from the officers. Eventually, Colston punched one officer and knocked him to the ground, then wrestled over a club with the other officer until he too was on the ground. Colston fled but did not get very far. One of the officers drew his gun and shot Colston twice in the back. Colston was charged with two counts of assaulting a police officer.

The Athens, Texas, jury that heard the case deliberated for twenty-three hours before convicting Colston of a lesser charge and recommending that he not be imprisoned. Albert Rodriguez, a Texas training officer, testified that the whole situation occurred "because Colston resisted arrest." Rodriguez said the force was justified, "In order to control the situation, the officers had to use force. That's the only alternative they've got." Colston, on the other hand, believed that the officer had no reason to arrest him and that he had acted in self-defense. Texas law allows a suspect to use self-defense against police using excessive force.

As in the Colston case, it is common for a police officer to perceive a suspect as having provoked an incident. Experts caution that police brutality typically is not planned or premeditated. "The truth," Paul Chevigny wrote in *Police Power: Police Abuses in New York City*, "is that many incidents of the use of force by policemen bear an unfortunate resemblance to assaults by private citizens; they are hotheaded reactions to a real or imagined insult." Regardless of why they cross the line, however, officers who use excessive force are harming citizens, not protecting and serving them.

4

Brutality by Race

THE ISSUE OF RACE is a constant theme in discussions of police brutality. Many concerned citizens charge that police brutality is far more likely to occur against black people than any other group. When MTV asked rapper Ice Cube to comment on the Rodney King beating, Cube replied, "It's been happening to us for years. It's just we didn't have a camcorder every time it happened."

The late novelist and essayist James Baldwin once said it is hard to find a black American "from the most circumspect church member to the most shiftless adolescent, who does not have a long tale to tell of police incompetence, injustice, or brutality."

One of the problems that arises in most discussions of the relationship between police brutality and race is the lack of hard data. Few comprehensive studies have been done, and few government agencies or police departments organize their records so that complaints based on race are easily gathered. The lack of statistics is not limited to race-related brutality.

Brutality in general is difficult to document. When brutal police behavior does occur, it is rarely in front of witnesses. As a rule, only the accused and the accuser are present. Attorney

(Opposite page) A demonstrator protests the brutal police beating of Rodney King. His sign expresses the view that minorities are more often the targets of such beatings.

Paul Chevigny, who conducted one of the most detailed studies of police abuse of power in the 1960s, found this to be the case. In *Police Power* he included only cases that could be documented by a witness or evidence besides the testimony of those directly involved.

Despite the limits Chevigny placed on his study, he concluded that police abuse is more common against blacks and Latinos than against other groups. This view has been expressed by many different people, including Wade Henderson of the NAACP. During a congressional hearing held in April 1991, Henderson said:

> For too long, African Americans and other racial minorities have been among the special targets of police abuse. Rather than being the beneficiaries of the equal protection of the law, too often innocent black people—including many of our youngsters—find themselves the victims of the abuse of authority and law.

Henderson described some of the behavior that leads blacks, in particular, to conclude that police target them for abuse because of their race:

> Some police officers, for example, make plain their fear or contempt of black people while on patrol in black communities or when they observe African Americans in predominantly "white areas" of our cities and towns. This is usually done through simple harassment or verbal abuse directed at an individual because of the color of his skin.

Local offices of the NAACP often hear from black people who feel they have been subjected to excessive force by police. According to Henderson, black citizens commonly report that

> white policemen, in particular—whether because of racial fears or animosities, or other factors— frequently overreact in a given circumstance. They use excessive force in situations which require deliberate, careful, and even-handed policing. The result is often severe injury or death for the victim of this abuse.

Harrington/People's Daily World.

"Well, chief, we didn't actually see him doing anything.
But he's black and he was walking real fast."

Even when statistics are available, their meaning is not always clear. In Los Angeles, for example, 41 percent of the brutality complaints come from black residents, although black people make up only 13 percent of the city's population. These numbers suggest to some that police brutality is more common in black communities than elsewhere. However, the same statistics could also mean that black people report brutality at a higher rate than other groups or that, in Los Angeles, police have a higher rate of contact with black crime suspects. The numbers alone also do not indicate whether the alleged abuse was racially motivated.

Most people, including many police officers,

Black gang members are arrested in Los Angeles. While police officers acknowledge that some racists exist within their ranks, some experts caution against oversimplifying the relationship between race and brutality.

would probably agree that some officers are racists and that their actions on the street reflect their personal views. In this respect, at least, police are no different from the general public, which exhibits a wide variety of ideas, biases, and interests. However, some police experts caution against oversimplifying the relationship between race and brutality.

The failure of leadership within a police agency and department policies regarding use of force may play a larger role in brutality than an individual officer's racist views. These two factors were at the heart of what happened to Rodney King, according to Edwin J. Delattre, author of *Character and Cops*. In an article in the *Washington Post Weekly Edition*, Delattre writes:

> Such profound failures of supervision—and of integrity, judgment, and professional competence— cannot be accounted for simply by racism. Neither

can they be attributed entirely to deficiencies in police training, nor to a shortage of "sensitivity" training of police in the customs and values of minority groups. . . . When police go this wrong, they are completely out of touch with the ideals of justice, freedom, and professionalism.

Brutal legacy

No explanation of why brutality occurs can ease the hurt or right the wrong suffered by those who, because of their race, have experienced brutality at the hands of police. Brutality by race has existed in American society for generations. From the nation's infancy to the twentieth century, this violence was most likely to be focused against black men and was often sanctioned or administered by police or people given policing powers. White slave holders gave police power to bands of poor white men and allowed them to enter slave quarters in the night and beat black slave families with sticks as they slept. After the Civil War, brutality against blacks continued. Sometimes groups like the Ku Klux Klan led the violence. Often, local police ignored these activities; sometimes they participated. Although this kind of violence was more common in the South, it also occurred in the North, especially after huge numbers of black people migrated to northern cities and the West Coast in the early twentieth century.

Police brutality against black people has been well documented at many points in recent U.S. history, too. In the 1960s, commissions in Newark, Detroit, Los Angeles, and other cities investigated relations between police and black people following outbreaks of racial rioting. The commissions heard testimony from community members about police abuse and concluded that police abuse did exist and was directed, at least in part, on the basis of race. Amnesty International,

Harrington/People's Daily World.

"I'd love to join you boys tonight, but we got to bust up an unlawful meetin' of Blacks in town."

a group concerned with physical abuse by governments against citizens, investigated law enforcement practices in Los Angeles following the beating of Rodney King in March 1991 and said: "The evidence suggests that racial minorities, particularly Blacks and Latinos, have been subjected to discriminatory treatment and are disproportionately the victims of abuse."

Many respected black citizens and members of the nation's other minority groups tell of brutal encounters with police that they believe took place because of their race. Baseball Hall of Famer Joe Morgan, Los Angeles Laker Jamal Wilkes, California congressman Melvyn Dymally, Detroit physician Walter Evans, Boston

Firefighters turn a hose on black citizens during a 1963 civil rights demonstration. Many black Americans claim that they are treated more brutally by police because of their race.

Celtic Dee Brown, and actor Blair Underwood have all accused police officers of treating them brutally because they are black.

Brutality by race is also confirmed by experiences of black police officers. Detroit police lieutenant K. D. Bullock, who has served on the force for more than two decades, still remembers his own encounter with police brutality. In the 1950s, Bullock explains, Detroit police frequently used unlawful force against young black males. Bullock was thirteen years old and on his way home from church when four officers called him over, then closed the squad car window on his tie. The officer driving the car said, "Let's see how fast he can run," and started moving the vehicle. Bullock recalls in a 1992 article in *Essence* that police abused blacks regularly. "If you challenged the police, as a Black man, you got into trouble," he says. "We were always taught to stay out of trouble. Police didn't like to see too many Black boys together. My parents had four boys and we went to the grocery store two at a time. That's the way things were."

Baseball Hall of Famer Joe Morgan accused police of brutal treatment.

Although many prominent black leaders have spoken out about their personal experiences with racial brutality, most believe that change will not happen until elected political leaders take action. The race problem is compounded when it is ignored by political officials outside police departments. Local politicians, as the decision makers outranking the police chief in most cities, have the power to demand changes in policy and practice. Some local politicians, black and white, do respond to concerns about brutality and take actions to investigate charges and make reforms as necessary. But some white politicians may be less sensitive to the problem of police brutality against black people and other racial or ethnic groups.

A breakdown in race relations

Many local black leaders blamed white politicians for the breakdown in race relations that occurred over the case of Rev. Lee Johnson. Johnson was a student minister in April 1983, serving Brooklyn's Concord Baptist Church while he studied at the prestigious Union Theological Seminary. Two police officers in Harlem stopped him for not having a front license plate. The officers began the encounter with racial name-calling; then they arrested Johnson, handcuffed him, and charged him with resisting arrest and disorderly conduct. The officers took Johnson to the police station, and in the basement there, beat him up.

Black community leaders called for a quick response. What they got was disappointing at best; some used the words "insulting" and "irresponsible." When Mayor Ed Koch heard of Johnson's story, he said, "I find it certainly possible, but nevertheless strange, that in the heart of Harlem, two white cops would intentionally, in violation of the law, harass a minister." To many listeners, Koch's comment implied that the mayor did not believe the minister's statement about the circumstances of his arrest. In an article in the *New Yorker*, writer Andy Logan pointed out that interpreted in this fashion, Koch's response was deeply offensive "in a black community where religious leaders continue to be awarded the power and respect that they have largely lost in other neighborhoods."

Reverend Johnson's situation attracted the attention of Congress, which feared that the news coming out of Queens was a sign of systematic police brutality by race in New York City. Michigan representative John Conyers Jr., who was on the Criminal Justice Subcommittee of the House Judiciary Committee in 1983, thought the situation was so serious that he arranged to hold congressional hearings about the allegations of police brutality in New York City.

The public speaks

Representative Conyers and his subcommittee were overwhelmed by the response from local residents wanting desperately to be heard. So many people asked to speak that the subcommittee had to schedule an additional session. Residents eventually related nearly a hundred stories of racially motivated police brutality in New York City. These hearings helped bring about some change in America's most populous city and the nation's largest police force. For one, the NYPD hired Benjamin Ward, its first black police commissioner.

Concerned about the apparent prevalence of police abuses, Conyers's subcommittee held investigative hearings in other cities where large numbers of complaints were filed against police officers. Conyers's experience in hearings in Los

Mayor Ed Koch swears in Benjamin Ward as New York City's new police commissioner in 1983. The choice of a black man as police commissioner was meant to quell complaints of race-based attacks by police.

Angeles, Washington, D.C., Miami, and again in New York City during the second half of the 1980s influenced his sharp opinions about police abuse in the United States. Conyers believes that on the part of police, "There is discourtesy and basic disrespect for the citizen-law enforcement relationship." In particular, he says, many officers have little respect for the nation's black and Latino citizens. "They [the police officers] don't start off saying, 'I'm going to shoot a black citizen tonight,' but they carry an attitude with them that leads to that."

Race as probable cause

Police can legitimately stop anyone for probable cause, and some black leaders believe that a black person is more likely to be stopped than a white person. "Probable cause" means that reasonable suspicion exists that a person has committed a crime. An officer who has reasonable grounds to believe a person has committed a crime can make an arrest and search the person; after the arrest, the officer can also search the vehicle or part of the room in which a person is arrested. Furthermore, police can stop and frisk a person for conduct that is suspicious but does not by itself justify arrest. "Suspicious conduct" is defined by a person's appearance, demeanor, and actions. It might include unusual behavior, acting nervous or talking nervously when questioned, or walking fast.

For police to stop someone as "suspicious" on the basis of race, however, is a violation of the constitutional right of equal protection under the law.

Many observers fear that police nevertheless use race as a reason to define a person as suspicious. Writer Les Payne, who believes this to be the case, has discussed the subject in *Essence:* "The underlying truth is that, despite the decades of enormous black success and achievement, police continue to view black skin itself as 'probable cause.'"

Such attitudes and actions by police do not necessarily amount to brutality. Yet they raise the level of tension, distrust, and even hostility between police and the community. Though this

Many minorities charge that police will stop and hassle them for no reason. Here, Washington, D.C., police frisk a black drug suspect.

does not automatically lead to brutality, abuse of police power is more likely to occur in an atmosphere of tension, distrust, and hostility.

One of the best-known cases of police using race as probable cause occurred in San Diego in the early 1970s. San Diego police arrested Edward Lawson, a black man, fifteen times in five years. Lawson, who worked as a disk jockey and promoter of rock concerts, was in his mid-thirties and wore his hair in dreadlocks. Police repeatedly arrested Lawson as he walked through a middle-class white neighborhood because they said he looked "suspicious."

Lawson challenged the police department's right to stop him repeatedly and ask for identification during his walks. He perceived the police department's actions as harassment and routinely refused to provide identification to police. He was prosecuted twice for failing to provide identification and on one of those occasions was convicted. In 1983, in *Kolender v. Lawson*, the U.S. Supreme Court ruled in Lawson's favor. Experts caution, however, that Lawson's case has done relatively little to stop some officers from harassing black people who are suspected because of their race.

In the 1970s, Edward Lawson was arrested fifteen times by officers because he looked "suspicious." Such treatment prompted criticism that arrests of blacks are racially motivated.

Many observers believe that to stop racially motivated police abuses, society itself must change. They suggest that police departments often merely reflect the racism found in American culture. The culture, and police, have made significant progress in race relations in the last century, but racism still exists in the United States.

If police departments are to overcome this problem, they will need to open a serious dialogue on the issues of race and brutality. Gerald Williams believes that discussion must occur before there can be any progress:

> There must be a frank discussion of racial issues internally and externally as they relate to our police departments all across the country. We must confront in a much more direct way than many of us have in the past the issues of racism in our organizations and how it affects our interactions with individual citizens and the greater community. We need to establish an environment in our police organizations in which both male and female officers of all races and ethnic groups can talk about these issues in an open and honest way.

Demonstrators protesting the acquittal of police officers in the Rodney King case draw a connection between racism and brutality.

5

Results of Brutality

POLICE BRUTALITY harms its individual victims and the community at large. It damages the image of police and of the criminal justice system and disrupts law and order. It destroys trust between police and people in the community and alienates members of the groups who feel they are singled out for abusive behavior rather than protection by the police.

The harms to society are difficult to measure. One can calculate property damage caused in a riot, but one cannot calculate the human frustration and despair that led to the riot. One can count the number of complaints filed against police officers, but one cannot count the number of times police officers have perjured themselves to cover up police brutality. Although measuring the harm of police brutality is elusive, its effects can easily be viewed through some of the fundamental damage it causes.

(Opposite page) The worst incidents of public rioting have been provoked, in part, by incidents of police brutality. Rioters loot stores in Los Angeles following the acquittal of officers in the Rodney King beating trial.

Public chaos

One of the peculiar effects of police brutality is rioting. Rioting has a long, extensive history in the United States. Indeed, police departments in many cities were originally formed to combat rioting. Rioting in the 1960s and later has followed a pattern of response to incidents of police brutality.

The worst incidents of public rioting—including riots in Detroit, Newark, and the Watts and South-Central sections of Los Angeles—were provoked, in part, by police brutality. Researchers found police practices to be the primary grievance of rioters, followed by social conditions—unemployment and poor housing. George Edwards, a former judge and Detroit police commissioner, believed that routine police brutality by race created a hostile climate between the black community in Detroit and the police, which he predicted would lead to a riot. This is how Edwards described the Detroit situation in 1965:

> Although local police forces generally regard themselves as public servants with the responsibility of maintaining law and order, they tend to minimize this attitude when they are patrolling areas that are heavily populated with Negro citizens. There, they tend to view each person on the streets as a potential criminal or enemy, and all too often that attitude is reciprocated. Indeed, hostility between the Negro communities in our large cities and the police departments is the major problem of law enforcement in this decade. It has been a major cause of all recent race riots.

Rioting broke out in Detroit two years later, in 1967, triggered by an incident of police brutality. The Newark race riot in the same year was due to the same cause. Police in the New Jersey city had stopped cab driver John Smith for tailgating and, during the contact, they kicked him and beat him, breaking several ribs and aggravating a hernia. They also kicked the left side of the black man's head hard enough to leave a gaping hole. Police then transported Smith to the precinct house, where one reporter

stated "he was again beaten, kicked, and had his head dunked in a toilet bowl."

Within a few hours of Smith's arrest, an angry, but peaceful, protest began outside the station house. Later in the evening, demonstrators began throwing bricks and rocks. Near midnight, someone threw a couple of Molotov cocktails at the station house wall, and shortly after that widespread looting broke out. These incidents led to three days of rioting in which twenty people died and another thousand were injured. There were more than a thousand arrests.

Riots are an expression of intense community frustration, and one of the causes of frustration most often cited by rioters is police brutality. Police brutality is such a suffocating form of oppression that some members of the community may see no other way to express their frustration than by rioting. In *Police Power*, researcher Paul

The 1967 Newark race riot broke out in response to a brutal beating of a black man. A man caught looting and burning a building during the riot lies dead in the street, killed by police.

Chevigny wrote, "Police abuse and consequent conviction [of suspects] on false evidence are a combination which feeds the impulse to riot; once respect for the legal process is gone, grievances can be expressed only by force."

Rioting often leads to a show of force—sometimes excessive force—by police. Because riots are, by definition, mass lawlessness, immediate danger threatens the community and police alike. Police attempt to prepare for such danger by arriving on the scene in riot gear, which includes crash helmets, clubs, and chemical weapons such as tear gas or Mace. The tension created by rioting and a highly mobilized police response increases the likelihood of excessive force. Some state governments have chosen to stop rioting by calling out military troops, such as the National Guard, to combat their own citizens.

A riot devastates a community. It causes tremendous economic damage as well as physically and emotionally wounding residents. Economic recovery often takes years, or even decades, but trust and faith may take even longer to rebuild. Using military or paramilitary force against a community, even for the purpose of restoring order, can itself become a negative effect of the riot.

Police suited up in riot gear patrol the streets during riots in Washington, D.C., in 1991. Rioting was sparked by a police shooting of a Hispanic man.

Police brutality affects citizens' views of the police. Regardless of whether incidents or patterns of brutality lead to public rioting, when these incidents are well publicized, they frequently lead to loss of credibility of the police in the eyes of citizens. Many police officers are also upset because word of the brutality damages their professional image. Most officers have pride in the job they do and would not use excessive force, yet the actions of those who do have a negative effect on people's perceptions of all police.

Even police departments in areas that have had absolutely no complaints of brutality may suffer from images such as those broadcast in the videotaped beating of Rodney King. Congressman Michael Kopetski, from Oregon, said:

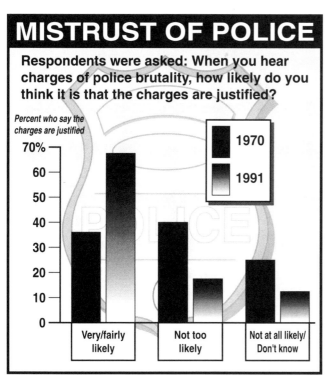

MISTRUST OF POLICE

Respondents were asked: When you hear charges of police brutality, how likely do you think it is that the charges are justified?

Percent who say the charges are justified

1970

1991

Very/fairly likely — Not too likely — Not at all likely/ Don't know

Source: CBS/New York Times poll, April 4, 1991.
Data provided by the Roger Center for Public Opinion Research, University of Connecticut, Storrs.

> I can tell you that officers there [in Oregon], they are mad about the Los Angeles situation and they are fearful that all police officers in this country will be branded with the same stroke, and fear that people will think in this country that all police officers are irresponsible and conduct illegal acts. We know that that is not the case.

Even the credibility of small town departments has suffered from this exposure. The police department of Bedminster Township, Pennsylvania, for example, has only five officers and has felt the backlash of the King videotape. Said Bedminster police chief David Stevens:

> We've never even had a police brutality suit in the history of our department, but you go into a restaurant and someone makes a comment about police brutality or jokes about police "batting practice." Even though this will pass and I know virtually all the citizens around here support us, it is unreal how the repetitious playing of this video has implanted these doubts and fears in many people's minds.

Rebuilding police image and community relations takes time and effort. Patrol Sergeant Nicholas Wade of Los Angeles believes this rebuilding was the most pressing issue facing his department after the King beating and the riots following the first verdict. "We have to reestablish our reputation with the community," said Wade. "Since the riots, since Rodney King, everyone basically has the same types of comments about the LAPD: What happened? What are you guys doing to get back to where you were?"

A bad police image is not healthy for a community. For a police department to function properly, the people it protects and serves must trust the department to be fair, decent, and lawful. Police brutality is none of those things. Instead, routine brutality encourages the community to distrust the machinery of law enforcement, to

doubt the word of the officers, and to suspect that other problems exist. Community members are less likely to feel confident in relying on the police to perform their jobs correctly.

Demonstrators protest police brutality in New York City.

Community relations

Systematic or frequent brutality also leads to adversarial relations with the communities subjected to the abuse. The Christopher commission, a panel that investigated brutality by the Los Angeles police following the Rodney King incident, recognized the strained relationship created by brutality. The commission noted that according to "a large number of witnesses . . . there is a general climate of hostility between the police and members of minority communities." When a community comes to believe that police are against them, they lose faith in the police department's ability and willingness to protect them and ensure their safety.

Police-community relations are most likely to become strained in areas where police frequently respond to calls for help, especially in lower-income neighborhoods. Ronald Hampton, a Washington, D.C., police officer, stated that poor neighborhoods are unique in that they have the highest rates of crime and are the most frequent users of 911 services, yet also experience the

Relations between police and residents suffer when police use excessive force. Protest signs illustrate the sense of frustration felt by residents of one community.

most incidents of police abuse. As Hampton points out:

> The National Black Police Association, our many members, and the community residents they work for have complained for years that they, the residents, were disrespected, disregarded, and physically and verbally abused, but they are the ones who uniquely call the police the most.

This concern is echoed by Richard Lacayo, who described this phenomenon in *Time* magazine:

> Law-abiding residents of crime-infested neighborhoods are desperate for police protection. They, after all, are the ones most likely to fall victim to muggers or drive-by shooters. But they also want the police's use of force to be kept in check, especially in poor neighborhoods where everyone is apt to be treated like a suspect.

These tensions in police-community relations have many side effects. The community may become less likely to report crime or cooperate with police investigations. Members of a brutalized community may become openly hostile to police. In 1985, eighteen-year-old Steven Whittingham told a reporter that victims of repeated police abuse can build up enough anger to strike back. Whittingham, a resident of New York, said, "I know a group of kids who're tired of it, who wanna kill a cop."

Easing tensions

Many police departments are concerned about tensions in the areas they serve. Law enforcement agencies have tried to rebuild or improve community relations by changing the way police perform their jobs. Some have increased the use of volunteer organizations, such as Neighborhood Watch, which are effective not only in assisting with crime prevention but also in creating a partnership between the police and citizens. Departments have put officers back in regular daily contact with people who live and work in the neighborhoods. "Let them know what really goes on out here," said one foot patrol officer. "You get to know these people, and after a while, you're not just a police officer. You owe them something more."

Justice system corruption

The justice system also suffers from the presence of police brutality. Here corruption most often occurs in the form of perjured testimony. Perjury is the giving of false testimony under oath, either by outright lying or by not honoring one's sworn commitment to tell "the whole truth." Throughout the history of police brutality, including present-day cases, police perjury has been common. Perjury in these situations may range from falsely denying the use of force to filing false charges against victims.

When false evidence and perjured testimony are admitted into the state and federal courts, the prosecutors, defense attorneys, and judges, wittingly or not, become part of the tainted system. Harvard law professor and prominent defense attorney Alan Dershowitz believes that court personnel should be more diligent in determining the truthfulness of police statements in cases involving excessive force. Dershowitz writes that "the primary responsibility for the pervasiveness of police perjury lies squarely with those prosecutors who close their eyes to it and with those judges who pretend to believe it."

On the other hand, attorney Paul Chevigny points out in *Police Power* that the local prosecutor can be "a hero behind the scene," although it does not always happen. Chevigny argues that when prosecutors use their power properly, they can correct some police abuses, especially the

Police patrol a neighborhood on foot. Many people believe that police brutality would occur less often if officers had closer contact with members of the communities they serve.

filing of false charges. He observes:

> The District Attorney has enormous power to correct police abuses—more power, perhaps, than the courts themselves—by refusing to prosecute when police testimony is doubtful or when the defendant's case is overwhelmingly strong. Nothing can put a stop to abuse more quickly than a refusal to prosecute.

Police officers have learned that filing false charges is the best defense against an accusation of brutality. Police are more likely to be able to justify their use of force if they arrest the victim. Almost every citizen who is injured by excessive force is charged with resisting arrest, disorderly conduct, felonious assault, or some similar charge. Sometimes the victim has in fact committed these offenses, but not always. Fundamentally, the victim is charged to discredit him or her as a law-abiding citizen and to strengthen the officer's case for needing to use force.

Although the initial brutality incident may have been wrong, it was not likely to have been

Lawyer Alan Dershowitz blames the frequency of police perjury in court on prosecutors. He believes it is up to prosecutors to root out and eliminate such perjury.

planned. The filing of false charges and perjury, however, are seen by Paul Chevigny as premeditated illegal acts. "The false criminal charges," he says, "are a more serious offense by a patrolman and constitute a greater evil than the act of violence itself."

Not only do these acts harm the judicial system, they harm police credibility in general, with the result that people will be less likely to believe police officers, even when they testify under oath. In *Above the Law: Police and the Use of Excessive Force*, police scholars Jerome Skolnick and James Fyfe documented the extent to which police credibility and community relations suffer when police are perceived as liars. They cite the example of a university professor who sat on a jury in Oakland, California: "He was dismayed that a defendant, whom he believed to be guilty [of murder], had been acquitted because

Police subdue a drug suspect. Police must walk a fine line between reasonable and excessive use of force.

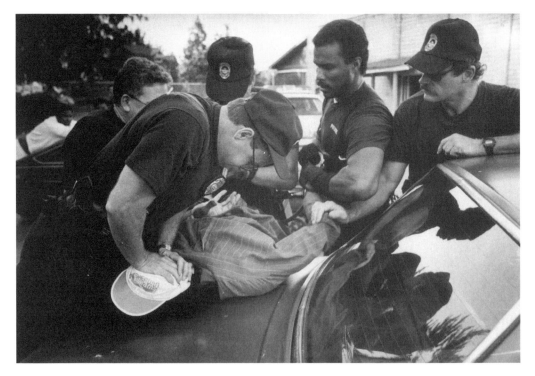

most of the jurors did not believe the police, even about how long it takes to drive from west to east Oakland."

Breakdown of law and order

For most citizens, the disturbing presence of police brutality raises the question: If the officers do not obey the law, then who will? Our society is based on the idea that the citizens agree collectively to obey the law. In America, police are supposed to identify and arrest people who do not obey the law. When the police themselves disobey the law, this social contract, or fundamental agreement of how people are to act, has broken down.

When police brutality is left unchecked in this country, it harms us all in many ways. A society that permits police brutality promotes corruption and lawlessness in every area of law enforcement, violating the Constitution and trashing the concept of rule by law. Periodic well-publicized incidents of police brutality alienate entire groups of people who are citizens and threaten public order. Systematic police brutality endangers the very foundations of our society.

6

Remedies

STOPPING POLICE BRUTALITY in America has proven difficult. Despite awareness of the problem since the early days of police departments, citizens have not been able to make it go away. Investigations by commissions from the 1930s to the 1990s produced concrete suggestions to reduce brutality. Many of these suggestions have been tried, though not all of them have been effective.

Because brutality still occurs, responsible citizens continue to look for solutions. Some police departments have made significant improvements, and other cities can look to these models as guides. Police department reforms, legal pressure, media exposure, and citizen interest can all help to further reduce police brutality.

Resort to courts

The high cost of resolving brutality complaints is currently driving debate about police reform. Costs are incurred at many stages during a claim of brutality. Complaints against the police must be investigated. If the victim files a lawsuit, the city must either negotiate a resolution or go to trial, paying investigative costs and legal fees, and funding jury verdicts and settlements if these are awarded.

(Opposite page) Solutions to police brutality have not come easily. But police departments and the citizens they serve continue to work for reforms.

Jury verdicts and settlements can be extremely costly. In 1987 a Detroit jury awarded more than a million dollars to Rufus Steward, who suffered permanent injuries including brain damage after being beaten by police who had stopped him for alleged drunk driving. In another case, Oklahoma City agreed to pay up to $830,000 to settle the brutality case of Joe Dean Shaw. Shaw suffered facial fractures as a result of being struck by police who had stopped him for a traffic violation in April 1984.

Increasing pressure and scrutiny

Jury awards like these sometimes motivate taxpayers and their elected representatives to pressure local police departments to stop brutality. These expenses, which have risen to millions of dollars for some cities in recent years, have brought about greater political scrutiny of the police. The City of Los Angeles, for example, paid more than $20 million in brutality claims between 1986 and 1990. And in 1994, Rodney King won $3.8 million in his lawsuit against the city. Government dollars are needed for roads, social services, and public safety, so taxpayers get upset when the money is used to pay for police misconduct.

Legal action does not always produce needed change, however. Drew Days handled numerous brutality complaints before becoming an assistant attorney general in the Clinton administration. He has written:

> What I found was that even though we brought successful damage actions against police departments for police brutality . . . there appeared to be no change in the environment, no change in the context in which police officers worked. There seemed to be no discipline from the top. There seemed to be no criticism by police or city officials of officers who were found to have engaged in police misconduct.

The city of Los Angeles paid a high price, financially and emotionally, for the actions of Lawrence Powell (center) and another officer convicted in the beating of Rodney King.

Police brutality lawsuits sometimes help just by making the problem more visible to the community. The publicity associated with a lawsuit also focuses public attention on the problem. Media attention in particular sometimes produces greater scrutiny over the department by elected officials. The city may also create a commission to review police practices and make recommendations for change. The lawsuits and other legal action often inspire public demand for an end to abuse of police authority. Although lawsuits have the potential to bring about change, most observers believe more incentive to eliminate brutality is necessary.

Former San Jose police chief Joseph McNamara believes a key remedy for police brutality is to improve police self-image. He said to Nikki Meredith:

> We tell our police officers that they are professionals, just like doctors or lawyers or psychologists. We tell them they need to remain objective about their work even when someone is terribly unfair and angry at them. It's understandable to get angry, but we are saying they are better than the average person in their ability to maintain calm and cool. That's what they're paid for.

A police trainee takes part in exercises. Police training often includes coursework on criminal procedure, emergency response, domestic violence, and use of weapons.

Police officers may receive training from several sources. Some officers attend college and earn degrees in criminal justice. Many attend a law enforcement training academy. Almost all police departments require on-the-job field training for rookie officers. More senior officers may also seek additional training opportunities from state and federal agencies.

Most states require that officers have a certain amount of classroom training, usually 120 to 180 hours. This basic academy work includes topics such as criminal procedure, statutory crimes, weapons training, emergency response, disaster preparedness, domestic violence, and controlled substances. The topics vary slightly from one academy to another, as does the amount of time spent on a topic. In some areas, for example, domestic violence will be covered in one hour, while another academy will spend three or four hours training officers to respond to domestic calls.

Many police reformers have called for additional training hours in civil rights and stress management to help prevent police brutality. The FBI trains approximately a thousand administrative-level officers annually at its facilities in Quantico, Virginia. In this twelve-week course, the officers receive a four-hour block on civil rights and a four-hour block on high-stress situations. The FBI also provides a similar, but shorter, training seminar to about four thousand law enforcement officers each year. Many police professionals believe that while these training experiences are helpful, they are not enough to stop the problem.

For example, Colorado police chief Gerald Williams believes that training intended to prevent police brutality should focus on improving verbal skills:

> Officers should receive training in the merits and the use of negotiations as a primary tool in response to confrontation. When an officer can negotiate a solution, he or she is less likely to utilize force as an immediate response to a crisis.

Discipline

Greater supervision of officers is another needed reform, and those who use excessive force must be disciplined. A common complaint

A police officer practices his aim at the FBI training facility in Quantico, Virginia.

is that officers accused of brutality who have been proven guilty in a court of law get promoted instead of fired. Many departments fail to adequately discipline officers for incidents of brutality and other kinds of abuse. Police experts, especially former officers, believe that appropriate discipline is perhaps the most important step in solving the problem of police brutality.

At the San Jose Police Department, discipline is used not just for punishing officers, but as a primary preventive measure. San Jose even disciplines officers for name-calling. Former chief McNamara, who set the tone, recalls:

> I worked in Harlem as a street officer for 10 years, and I never called anyone a name. If the public can't tell the difference between the good guys and the bad guys, then we're lost. And yes, we do discipline police for using foul language. Again and again we say, "How can you feel [that you're] better than the people who break the laws if you break the rules? You may think it's perfectly reasonable to call someone an asshole, but the public is shocked and so are juries. They expect more from police officers."

Integration

Historically, police departments in most cities have hired almost exclusively white male officers. In the past thirty years or so, however, departments have taken on more minorities and women. One reason for this is a series of laws passed during the 1960s that banned local governments from discriminating in employment, including the hiring of police officers. In addition, brutality complaints decrease when departments are better integrated. Consequently, many people seeking to eliminate police brutality and to promote understanding between police and the community also try to raise minority representation in the department.

Commissions formed to look at causes of racial rioting in Newark, Kansas City, Detroit, Los Angeles, and several other cities said that the lack of black police officers was one of the factors frustrating the rioters. Departments with few black officers alienated the black community and created distrust of police in general. Many cities instituted recruitment programs to increase the number of minorities that were hired for police work.

In addition to hiring more black and women officers, departments were pushed to promote minorities and hire them in leadership positions. When the riots of the mid-1960s broke out, no major American city had a black chief of police. By the early 1990s, more than a dozen black police chiefs or commissioners were in major police departments. Most American police departments have not fully integrated, but they have made significant progress. Many departments

Although most police departments are not fully integrated, many departments have worked hard to build forces that reflect the diversity of their communities.

today do a much better job of reflecting local ethnicity, hiring Asians, Latinos, and other minorities if these are present in the community as well.

Civilian review

Civilian review is another method of increasing police accountability. Currently, many departments investigate complaints of brutality themselves. Critics allege that self-review is ineffective and likely to lead to a cover-up. These analysts believe that an outside source is needed to provide fair and accurate investigation of the facts and to determine whether each alleged wrongdoing occurred as stated in the related complaint.

Police departments frequently resist efforts to establish civilian review boards. Most departments have internal review procedures, and many have full-time internal affairs investigators. Police argue that they, not civilians, are trained to investigate criminal charges. They particularly resent the implication that they cannot police themselves. In addition, police often believe that civilians do not understand the job of police officers and therefore are not qualified to judge whether an officer acted appropriately in a given situation. In many cities, efforts to establish

Police and citizens do not always agree on the best way to review complaints of police brutality.

civilian review have met organized political opposition from the police.

New York City became concerned about repeated reports of police brutality, perjury, corruption, and harassment in the 1960s. The police commissioner added four civilians to the three-member review board, making the civilians the majority voice. The Patrolmen's Benevolent Association (PBA), which passionately opposed this move, organized a referendum to place the civilian review on the ballot. The police actively campaigned against civilian review, arguing that it limits police ability to maintain order. Voters declined the civilian presence in the referendum. New York City again tried to create civilian review more than twenty years later. Nearly ten thousand officers blocked the Brooklyn Bridge in the fall of 1992 to protest the possibility of an all-civilian review board.

Types of civilian review board

The ACLU identifies three basic types of civilian review board. Type 1 is an independent and truly civilian board. Investigators for the board are not officers. The investigators submit their reports to a board of civilians, not officers. The civilian group then makes recommendations for action to the police chief. Police object most to all-civilian boards because such bodies are least able to balance negative facts brought out in investigations against the demands of police work. The ACLU believes that this kind of board is most effective because it is most independent of police influence.

The other two types are less independent. Type 2 boards use police officers to investigate each complaint and submit a report to a civilian board. Type 3 boards use police officers to investigate the complaints and make recommendations for action to the police chief. Complainants who disagree with the recommendations can appeal to a board of civilians. Boards of these kinds are more common and are less objectionable to police, because trained officers are investigating the allegations.

Supporters say that civilian review boards are good because they bring about change in the process and procedure of filing grievances. In some cities, a victim must file his or her grievance at the police station; this requirement, however, may be intimidating enough to discourage many potential complaints. The police

Police protest the idea of a civilian review board. Many police believe that no one can fully understand an officer's actions except another officer.

Citizens express their support for a civilian review board, which they believe will improve police response to community concerns.

station also may seem to obstruct attempts to file complaints against officers. For example, Paul King reported the abuse of his brother Rodney the day after the beating. He had to wait about an hour to speak to an officer. Instead of filing Paul King's complaint, however, the officer told King that his brother was in big trouble for putting a police officer's life in danger. George Holliday, who recorded the King beating on video, went to the same station, to offer his videotape as evidence and to ask whether the motorist, unknown to him at the time as Rodney King, was OK. The officers failed to take his complaint or his video, so Holliday took the tape to a local television station.

Although a primary purpose of civilian review is to investigate complaints against the police, James Fyfe believes such boards are ineffective at curbing police abuse:

> A citizens' review board is really an unsatisfactory bandaid in a lot of ways. In fact, people don't sit on the kind of review board that will look at complaints without being on the city payroll. To the outsider, there are city employees who say that they're independent of the police department but who are adjudicating [settling cases involving] other city employees.

Fyfe argues that the ideal police review should be performed under the supervision and leadership of the police chief:

> There are police chiefs in this country who will conduct thorough investigations of all complaints and then release the results of their investigations publicly, detailing everything they've found, detailing all their conclusions, and inviting the complainant or members of the public to comment further.

When the situation is appropriately handled as described, Fyfe says, there is no need for civilian review.

Community activism

Civilian review can be accomplished unofficially by community activists. Harriet Walden involved herself in police abuses after her two sons were falsely arrested and roughed up in Seattle in 1993. The Seattle Police Department

Harriet Walden started Mothers Against Police Harassment, a citizen complaint group, after her two sons (pictured) were falsely arrested and roughed up by police.

had an internal investigations division, but many of the mothers in Walden's neighborhood believed that the internal unit was not professional and did not take citizen complaints seriously. Walden and her friends started Mothers Against Police Harassment.

Mothers Against Police Harassment is an advocacy group that has among its goals the establishment of an independent civilian review board. It is a multiracial group of more than sixty members, who operate a hotline around the clock, and a volunteer advocate, who researches each complaint. Although the group receives about forty calls per month, only two or three of the callers are willing to go through the formal complaint process.

In addition to supporting people in the complaint process, Mothers Against Police Harassment collects records. Walden says, "I think it's a good idea to have the complaints because eventually we'll be able to track the officers, and we can say, well, this officer has had ten complaints against him in the last year. Why is he still on the force?"

Future considerations

The ultimate remedy for police brutality in a democratic society rests with the citizens and their expectations for themselves and their police. It is the citizens who confer on the police the authority to use force. The police power, then, rests on the consent of the citizens. The citizens have the ultimate ability to demand changes and to require police officers to be accountable for their actions. As observer Fred Bruning wrote in *Maclean's*, "Police carry the nightsticks. We [citizens] give the orders."

Organizations to Contact

The following organizations provide services or information about police practices and administration, and incidents of brutality and other abuses. More information can be obtained directly from each organization.

American Civil Liberties Union (ACLU)
132 W. 43rd St.
New York, NY 10036
212-944-9800

The ACLU is a national organization that supports legal and educational efforts to protect and preserve the constitutional rights of individuals. The ACLU publishes a variety of materials, including some pamphlets and manuals specifically about police brutality.

COPWATCH
2022 Blake St.
Berkeley, CA 94704
510-548-0425

COPWATCH is a local organization that monitors police activity. Volunteers work to preserve citizens' rights and fair treatment under the law. COPWATCH has been concerned with rights of the homeless as well as other groups lacking broad-based community support.

International Law Enforcement Stress Association (ILESA)
5485 David Blvd.
Port Charlotte, FL 33981-2268

ILESA is an organization of police officers and other criminal justice professionals. Among the resources available from ILESA is its quarterly journal, *Police Stress*.

National Association for the Advancement of Colored People (NAACP)

4805 Mt. Hope Dr.
Baltimore, MD 21215
301-481-4100

The NAACP is a national organization concerned with civil rights and social conditions of black people. Its publication lists include several titles on police brutality.

National Association of Chiefs of Police (NACOP)

3801 Biscayne Blvd.
Miami, FL 33137
305-573-0070

A professional organization for police executives, the NACOP collects research and studies police issues. It publishes books and professional journals about policing.

National Black Police Association (NBPA)

3251 Mt. Pleasant St. NW
Washington, DC 20010
202-986-2070

The NBPA was organized in 1972 to create a network among minority police officers across the country. Among its top goals is improving relations between police departments and the community, and it has developed a strategy for community-oriented policing that it promotes through training and education.

National Coalition for Police Accountability (NCPA)

59 E. Van Buren, Suite 2418
Chicago, IL 60603
312-663-5392

The NCPA is a coalition of legal, advocacy, victims', minority police, and religious organizations. Its primary mission is to address issues of police abuse.

National Institute of Justice (NIJ)
U.S. Department of Justice
PO Box 6000
Rockville, MD 20850
800-533-8811

The NIJ researches and compiles reports on crime in the United States. The NIJ publication list is available through the National Criminal Justice Reference Service.

National Organization of Black Law Enforcement Executives (NOBLE)
908 Pennsylvania Ave. SE
Washington, DC 20003
202-546-8811

NOBLE is a professional organization for black law enforcement officials. Its primary goal is to improve the quality of police services for all citizens.

National Urban League
500 E. 62nd St.
New York, NY 10021
212-310-9000

The Urban League is a civil rights organization that focuses on the economic condition and the empowerment of black Americans.

Police Executive Research Forum (PERF)
2300 M St. NW, Suite 910
Washington, DC 20037
202-466-7820

PERF is a professional organization of police chiefs, primarily from large city police departments. It conducts research and consults on police management issues. PERF publishes position papers and policy statements on policing issues.

Police Foundation
1001 22nd St. NW, Suite 200
Washington, DC 20037
202-833-1460

The Police Foundation is a research and consulting organization. It sponsors research on innovative police programs and maintains an extensive publications list.

Police Watch: Police Misconduct Lawyer Referral Service (PMLRS)
611 S. Catalina, Suite 409
Los Angeles, CA 90005
213-387-3325

The PMLRS provides consultation and assistance in filing claims for damages against the police. It also conducts workshops and seminars on topics of police misconduct litigation.

Suggestions for Further Reading

Kim Bendheim, "On Being Busted by the L.A.P.D.: A Citizen's Complaint," *The Nation*, April 20, 1992.

Anthony Bouza, *The Police Mystique: An Insider's Look at Cops, Crime, and the Criminal Justice System.* New York: Plenum Press, 1990.

Jean Carey Bond, ed., *Fighting Police Abuse: A Community Action Manual.* New York: American Civil Liberties Union, 1992.

Paul Chevigny, "Let's Make It a Federal Case," *The Nation*, March 23, 1992.

———, *Police Power: Police Abuses in New York City.* New York: Pantheon Books, 1969.

Alexander Cockburn, "Beat the Devil: In the Shadow of Rodney King," *The Nation*, April 15, 1991.

William Dudley, ed., *Police Brutality*. San Diego, CA: Greenhaven Press, 1991.

Rick Hertzberg, "Washington Diarist: L.A. F/X," *The New Republic*, May 25, 1992.

George Howland Jr., "Mothers Take On the Police," *The Progressive*, August 1993.

Andrew Liberman, "Get Your Black Ass in the House," *The Progressive*, September 1986.

Nikki Meredith, "A Better Way in San Jose," *Psychology Today*, May 1984.

———, "Attacking the Roots of Police Violence," *Psychology Today,* May 1984.

Jill Nelson, "The Blacks and the Blues: A Special Report on Police Brutality," *Essence*, September 1985.

Les Payne, "Up Against the Wall: Black Men and the Cops," *Essence*, November 1992.

Jerome Skolnick and James Fyfe, "Why Police Officers Are Quick to Use Their Batons," *Los Angeles Times*, March 21, 1993.

Diane Weathers, "If You Are a Victim of Police Brutality. . . ," *Essence*, November 1992.

Additional Works Consulted

Melinda Beck, "New York's 'Bad Apples,'" *Newsweek*, May 6, 1985.

Fred Bruning, "The Enemy Is Us, Not the L.A. Police Force," *Maclean's*, April 15, 1991.

Patrick Buchanan, "Police Brutality and Popular Reaction," *Conservative Chronicle*, March 20, 1991.

Timothy Chou, "On the Beat," *Los Angeles Times*, September 30, 1992.

Marc Cooper, "Dum Da Dum-Dum," *The Village Voice*, April 16, 1991.

S. J. Diamond, "Lives on the Line," *Los Angeles Times*, October 2, 1993.

Faye Fiore and Miles Corwin, "Toll of Violence Haunts Families of Police Officers," *Los Angeles Times*, February 21, 1994.

Scott Harris, "Six Months Later, a Day on the Beat," *Los Angeles Times*, November 17, 1992.

William F. Jasper, "Keep Them Local, Keep Us Free," *The New American*, May 21, 1991.

Jet, "Black Wins $830,000 in Police Brutality Suit," July 21, 1986.

———, "Detroit Man Gets $1 Million in Police Brutality Case," May 4, 1987.

———, "White Officers Charged in Death of Black Louisiana Man," January 25, 1988.

Patricia A. Jones, "Ending Police Brutality," *Black Enterprise*, February 1985.

June Jordan, "The Truth of Rodney King," *The Progressive*, June 1993.

Robin D. G. Kelley, "Straight from Underground," *The Nation*, June 8, 1992.

David Kupelian, "The Most Stressful Job in America: Police Work in the 1990s," *New Dimensions*, August 1991.

Richard Lacayo, "Law and Disorder," *Time*, April 1, 1991.

Andy Logan, "Lift Every Voice," *The New Yorker*, August 22, 1983.

National Review, "Law Breakers and Law Makers," April 15, 1991.

The New Yorker, "Tales of the Tapes," October 12, 1992.

Donald F. Norris, *Police-Community Relations: A Program That Failed*. Lexington, MA: Heath, 1973.

Police Brutality: Hearings Before the Subcommittee on Civil and Constitutional Rights of the Committee on the Judiciary. Washington, DC: U.S. Government Printing Office, 1992.

Charles Reith, *A New Study of Police History*. London: Oliver and Boyd, 1956.

Harvey Schlossberg and Lucy Freeman, *Psychologist with a Gun*. New York: Coward, McCann & Geoghegan, 1974.

Richard A. Serrano, "A New Direction, a Long Road," Los Angeles Times, November 17, 1992.

Jerome Skolnick and David Bayley, *The New Blue Line: Police Innovation in Six American Cities*. New York: Free Press, 1986.

Jerome Skolnick and James Fyfe, *Above the Law: Police and the Excessive Use of Force*. New York: Free Press, 1993.

Index

About the Author

Kelly C. Anderson is a historian and an award-winning book designer. She is a coauthor of numerous social studies textbooks and state histories. She graduated from Columbia College in Missouri and studied law and history at the University of Missouri.

Picture Credits

Cover photo by © Gilles Peress/Magnum Photos, Inc.
AP/Wide World Photos, 9, 18, 22, 26, 44, 52, 68, 83
The Bettmann Archive, 12, 19
© John W. Emmons/Impact Visuals, 28
© Frank Fournier/Woodfin Camp & Associates, Inc., 36
© Robert Fox/Impact Visuals, 80
© Katz/S. Nicol/Woodfin Camp & Associates, Inc., 69
© Richard B. Levine, 86, 94
© Andrew Lichtenstein/Impact Visuals, 32
© T.L. Litt/Impact Visuals, 42
© Jeff Lowenthal/Woodfin Camp & Associates, Inc., 14
© Danny Lyon/Magnum Photos, Inc., 10
© Marlow/Magnum Photos, Inc., 53, 93
© David Maung/Impact Visuals, 58
© Alain McLaughlin/Impact Visuals, 56
© Gilles Peress/Magnum Photos, Inc., 71, 79
© Alon Reininger/Woodfin Camp & Associates, Inc., 82
Reuters/Bettmann, 46, 89
© Frances M. Roberts, 96, 97
© Loren Santow/Impact Visuals, 31
© Dana Schuerholz/Impact Visuals, 98
© Lester Sloan/Woodfin Camp & Associates, Inc., 72
© Ted Soqui/Impact Visuals, 8, 16, 40, 90
© Les Stone/Impact Visuals, 34
UPI/Bettmann, 6, 21, 35, 62, 65 (both), 70, 75, 76, 91
© Piet van Lier/Impact Visuals, 15, 84

DISCARDED

LEAD HIGH SCHOOL LIBRARY
320 S. MAIN ST.
LEAD, SD 57754-1548
6674-97